EDMONTOSAURUS

By Susan H. Gray

THE CHILD'S WORLD®
CHANHA   ESOTA

The Child's World

Published in the United States of America by The Child's World®
PO Box 326, Chanhassen, MN 55317-0326
800-599-READ
www.childsworld.com

Content Adviser:
Peter Makovicky,
PhD, Curator,
Field Museum,
Chicago, Illinois

Photo Credits: American Museum of Natural History Library: 18, 21 (#7737); Reproduced with permission, Canadian Museum of Nature, Ottawa, Canada: 10, 23; James L. Amos/Corbis: 5; Bob Krist/Corbis: 20; photo by Rick Wicker, all rights reserved, Image Archives, Denver Museum of Nature and Science: 7; Reproduced with permission of the Minister of Public Works and Government Services Canada, 2004 and Courtesy of Natural Resources Canada, photo #109384, Geological Survey of Canada: 15; Linda Hall Library of Science, Engineering & Technology: 19; The Natural History Museum, London: 4, 11, 13, 17, 24; Francois Gohier/Photo Researchers, Inc.: 6, 8; Tom McHugh/Photo Researchers, Inc.: 9; Chase Studio/Photo Researchers, Inc.: 26; Albert Copley/Visuals Unlimited: 12.

The Child's World®: Mary Berendes, Publishing Director

Editorial Directions, Inc.: E. Russell Primm, Editorial Director; Katie Marsico, Associate Editor; Ruth Martin, Line Editor; Judith Shiffer, Assistant Editor; Matt Messbarger, Editorial Assistant; Susan Hindman, Copy Editor; Melissa McDaniel, Proofreader; Olivia Nellums, Fact Checkers; Tim Griffin/IndexServ, Indexer; Dawn Friedman, Photo Researcher; Linda S. Koutris, Photo Selector

Original cover art by Todd Marshall

The Design Lab: Kathleen Petelinsek, Design and Page Production

Library of Congress Cataloging-in-Publication Data
Gray, Susan Heinrichs.
  Edmontosaurus / by Susan H. Gray.
    v. cm. — (Exploring dinosaurs)
  Includes bibliographical references and index.
  Contents: Time for a check-up—What is an Edmontosaurus?—Who discovered Edmontosaurus?—The incredible mummy—A huge family tree—Big changes at the K-T boundary.
  ISBN 1-59296-235-1 (lib. bdg. : alk. paper) 1. Edmontosaurus—Juvenile literature. [1. Edmontosaurus. 2. Dinosaurs.] I. Title.
  QE862.O65G7453 2005
  567.914—dc22   2003027056

TABLE OF CONTENTS

CHAPTER ONE

TIME FOR A CHECKUP!

Edmontosaurus (ed-MON-toe-SAWR-uhss) was enjoying an excellent afternoon meal. He had found a patch of tender, young pine trees. The dinosaur began calmly pulling off their branches and chewing up the twigs and needles. Suddenly, he bit down on something hard and jerked his head back. He worked the hard piece around in his mouth, then spit it out with the rest of his food.

He tore off another branch and continued chewing. Again his head jerked back. Again he coughed everything out onto the

Edmontosaurus *was a peaceful, slow-moving plant eater. Scientists believe it probably had excellent hearing, eyesight, and smell. These senses would have helped it to avoid predators.*

These prehistoric pine cones would have seemed like a tasty treat to a hungry Edmontosaurus! *The dinosaur's beak was perfect for gripping tough plant matter such as seeds, twigs, and pine needles.*

ground. He ripped a third tender branch from the tree. He managed

to swallow one mouthful, when, yeow! There it was again! Some-

thing like a short stick dropped from his mouth.

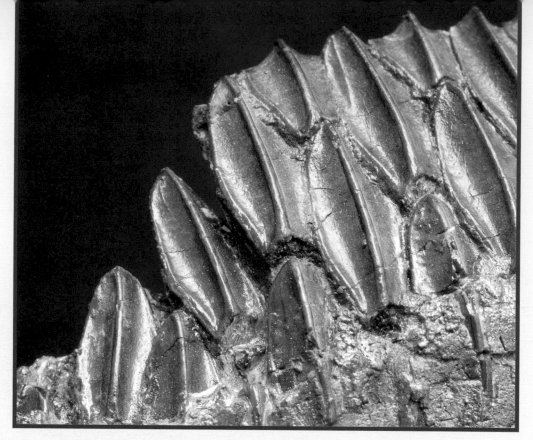

Meat eaters such as Tyrannosaurus rex *(tie-RAN-uh-SAWR-uhss REX) had razor-sharp teeth that were good for ripping and tearing.* Edmontosaurus, *on the other hand, had teeth that were flatter and better for grinding.*

Edmontosaurus was not getting an easy meal after all. And there on the ground were the clues to his problem. Three of his teeth had fallen out as he'd munched on the branches. Over the years, they had ground down hundreds of twigs and leaves, and it was time for them to go. New little teeth were growing in and pushing out the old ones.

Edmontosaurus paused for a little while. He nosed around the pine trees, then yanked off a large branch loaded with needles and cones. This time, he was not interrupted. He finished his meal and walked off.

This Edmontosaurus *skeleton is located at the Denver Museum of Nature and Science in Denver, Colorado.*

CHAPTER TWO

WHAT IS AN EDMONTOSAURUS?

Edmontosaurus was a dinosaur that lived from about 72 million to 65 million years ago. Its name is taken from words that mean "Edmonton lizard." Edmonton is the name of a city and a rock formation in Canada. *Edmontosaurus* was discovered in those rocks.

Edmontosaurus was a large dinosaur that grew to about 40 feet (12 meters) in length. Around half of that length was the animal's tail, which was thick and heavy, and not very **flexible.** The bones inside it did not allow the tail to bend.

This dinosaur bone bed makes up part of Dinosaur Provincial Park in Alberta, Canada. Scientists have found Edmontosaurus *remains in Canada, Wyoming, Alaska, Montana, and New Jersey.*

Edmontosaurus *could walk on its hind legs, but it also sometimes moved on all fours.*

Edmontosaurus weighed as much as 4 tons. It had thick, treelike legs that were much bigger than its arms. Its broad feet had three toes each. The arms were long enough for the dinosaur to lean forward and use them for walking. *Edmontosaurus* could also rear up

This skull once contained a brain that placed Edmontosaurus *somewhere in the middle when it came to dinosaur intelligence. Certain dinosaurs such as* T. rex *were smarter, but others such as* Stegosaurus *(STEG-oh-SAWR-uhss) were definitely less intelligent.*

and walk on its back legs.

The **reptile** probably could not run very fast, especially when using all four limbs.

Edmontosaurus's head was long and broad, with a blunt snout. A thick, hard **sheath** covered the upper lip. *Edmontosaurus* had no teeth at all in the front of its mouth, but its cheeks were jammed with hundreds of them. Each tooth was small and slender. Throughout its life, the dinosaur shed teeth as they wore out. Under each tooth was a column of three or four new teeth waiting to grow in.

A low ridge or frill ran down the center of the animal's back, from the head to the tip of the tail. *Edmontosaurus* had leathery skin that was covered with hard bumps, or tubercles (TOO-ber-kulz). Its tubercles were round, oval, or many-sided. Some were arranged in rows or patterns.

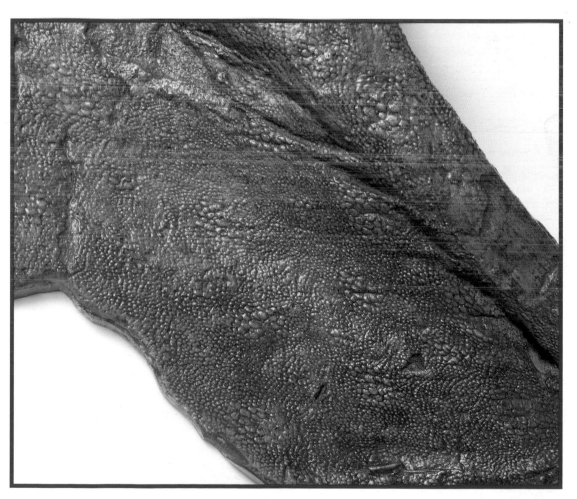

This fossilized skin once belonged to an Edmontosaurus. *Are you curious what* Edmontosaurus *skin felt like? Try touching a football!* Edmontosaurus *skin probably had the same bumpy, leathery texture.*

MAKING NOISES

Edmontosaurus had very large nostrils. Because of this, scientists believe it may have had some loose pouches of skin around its nose. The dinosaur might have been able to inflate the pouches like balloons. Perhaps it could even make sounds through them. But why would a dinosaur need to make sounds?

Animals make sounds for lots of reasons. Some animals cry out to warn others of danger. Warning cries are often loud and short so they can be heard easily and **interpreted**

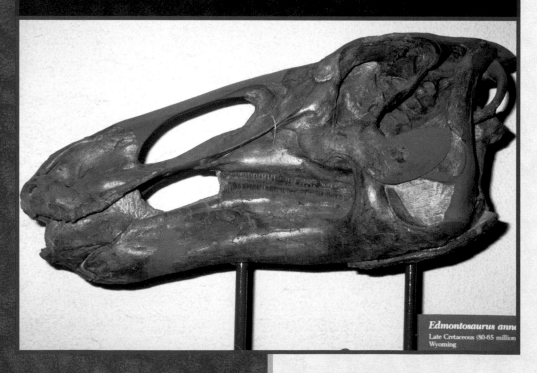

Edmontosaurus ann
Late Cretaceous (80-65 million
Wyoming

quickly. The warning calls of birds, for example, may be only one or two loud notes. Their regular songs, however, are often softer and more complex.

Sometimes animals make sounds to find mates. In the summertime, male elk make bellowing and whistling sounds. These sounds can attract female elk from far and wide.

Sometimes animals make sounds to scare enemies away. A tiger's roar, for example, tells attackers to keep their distance.

Edmontosaurus may have made sounds for any of these reasons. Maybe it honked its nose at enemies. Maybe it fluttered its nostrils to get a mate. Perhaps it blew up its pouches with one sound and then deflated them with another. Because we do not have a living *Edmontosaurus* to study, we may never know what sounds it made—or even if it made sounds at all.

CHAPTER THREE

WHO DISCOVERED EDMONTOSAURUS?

It's hard to say exactly who discovered *Edmontosaurus*. Lawrence Lambe, a Canadian scientist, named the dinosaur in a paper he wrote in 1917. But the dinosaur's remains may have been found 40, 50, or even 60 years earlier.

This dinosaur's story is quite confusing. To understand it, you must understand how paleontologists (PAY-lee-un-TAWL-uh-jists) work. Paleontologists are people who study fossils. Fossils are the remains of **ancient** plants and animals. They may be bones, footprints, seeds, or leaf imprints. Billions of plants and animals have lived on the earth. But not nearly that many have actually left fossils behind. Paleontologists try to understand things about ancient life with the fossils they have.

When paleontologists find a dinosaur fossil, they compare it to other fossils. They try to figure out where the new fossil fits in. Sometimes a new dinosaur fossil looks just like the fossil of a known dinosaur. Sometimes it looks similar to a known fossil, but not exactly the same. Sometimes it looks completely different. Sometimes it is so broken that it cannot even be compared to other fossils. It's not always easy to figure out where a new fossil fits in or which dinosaur

Canadian fossil hunter Lawrence Lambe was responsible for naming several dinosaurs. In 1923, the dinosaur Lambeosaurus (LAM-bee-oh-SAWR-uhss) was named in honor of the famous paleontologist.

it came from. This was the problem with *Edmontosaurus*.

One paleontologist found fossils and said they came from a dinosaur named *Claosaurus* (CLAY-oh-SAWR-uhss), the "broken lizard." Someone else found fossils that looked the same and said they came from *Edmontosaurus*. Another fossil hunter found similar remains and said they came from *Thespesius* (thess-PAY-zee-uhss), the "wondrous one." Still others found similar fossils and named them *Anatosaurus* (uh-NAT-oh-SAWR-uhss) and *Trachodon* (TRAY-koh-don). Things were getting more and more confusing. It was becoming impossible to tell which dinosaurs were which, and which fossils really came from *Edmontosaurus*.

Over time, some of those fossils turned out to be from known dinosaurs. Others seemed to be from new dinosaurs. One of the new dinosaurs was given the name *Edmontosaurus*. Even today, things

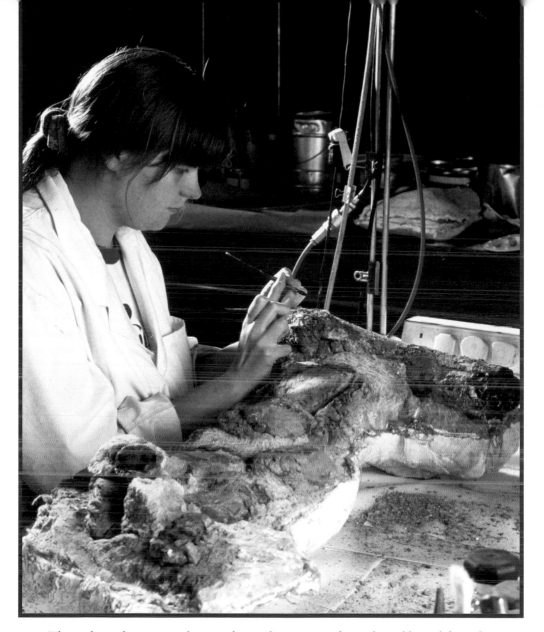

This paleontologist is working on bones that once made up the ankle and foot of an Edmontosaurus. Today, paleontologists are extremely careful when they handle the remains of ancient plants and animals. In the late 1800s and early 1900s, workers were not as cautious and accidentally damaged or destroyed several precious fossils.

aren't completely settled. Many of those fossils still aren't easy to

match with any dinosaur.

CHAPTER FOUR

THE INCREDIBLE MUMMY

One of the most amazing dinosaur fossils ever found was an *Edmontosaurus* discovered in 1909 in Wyoming. The skeleton was almost complete, with the bones in the same place as they would have been in life. Even more incredible was what the skeleton

Fossil hunter Charles Sternberg stands beside newly discovered dinosaur remains in the early 1900s. The Sternbergs were famous fossil hunters and were responsible for finding the Edmontosaurus *mummy.*

The Edmontosaurus *mummy was an exciting find for paleontologists. It helped them learn more about the dinosaur's skin, diet, and prehistoric environment.*

was wrapped in. Although the skin itself had rotted away years ago,

it had left its imprint on the sand around the dinosaur.

To the fossil hunters who found it, the dinosaur looked as if

it were lying on the ground, complete with its dried-up skin. It

appeared to be a dinosaur mummy. The animal's rib cage was spread and the head was drawn back. One of the discoverers wrote that the dinosaur "lay there with expanded ribs as in life, wrapped in the impressions of the skin. . . ." Looking carefully, they could make out beautiful patterns of eight-sided tubercles covering the skin.

The mummy's hands looked like mittens, with webs of skin between the fingers. Some scientists believe the "mittens" appeared after the dinosaur died, perhaps as skin began to slip from its hands.

The incredible mummy was gently moved from its grave in Wyoming. Great care was taken so that the skin impressions were not damaged.

Today, the *Edmontosaurus*

The American Museum of Natural History in New York is home to almost 1 million fossils, including the Edmontosaurus *mummy.*

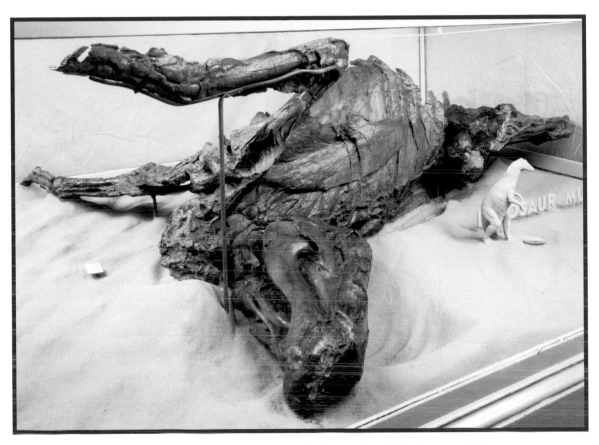

The Edmontosaurus *mummy is now on display in New York, but not all dinosaur fossils are available for public viewing. Some prehistoric remains are very fragile and are therefore kept in museum storage. Museum workers often use molds to create copies of these fossils, which are then put on display for visitors to study.*

mummy is on display at the American Museum of Natural History in New York. A second *Edmontosaurus* mummy much like the first one was also found in 1909. This second **specimen** is on display at the Senckenberg Museum in Frankfurt, Germany.

A FAMOUS FAMILY OF FOSSIL FINDERS

The *Edmontosaurus* mummy was discovered by some of the most famous fossil hunters ever—the Sternberg family. It all started with little Charles Sternberg (right). As a boy in New York, he loved hunting fossils. After his family moved to Kansas in 1867, he began finding fossils around his new home. Each find was so exciting that young Charles decided to hunt fossils for the rest of his life.

Charles seemed to have a sixth sense when it came to finding fossils. He seemed to find them wherever he went. Charles later had three sons who shared his interest— George, Charlie, and Levi. One day nine-year-old George visited his dad, who had set up camp in Kansas to hunt fossils. He wandered off for a little while and discovered the skeleton of an ancient swimming reptile. This was an exciting turning point for the boy. A few years later, he quit school so he could work full time with his father.

Charlie joined his dad and brother George when he was only 14. Together, the three hunted fossils for museums and schools. They found giant tortoises,

dinosaurs, and ancient mammals. Charlie was a true scientist and wrote many papers about these discoveries.

In time, Levi, the youngest son, also joined the team. Like his dad and brothers, he had a knack for knowing just where to look for dinosaurs. Levi loved working outdoors. Even on the hottest days, he was happy and cracking jokes.

The Sternbergs devoted their lives to fossil hunting. Together, they found tens of thousands of fossils. By the time they died, they had become famous throughout the United States and Canada for their many discoveries.

CHAPTER FIVE

A HUGE FAMILY TREE

Edmontosaurus was a hadrosaur (HAD-roe-SAWR), or duck-

billed dinosaur. The hadrosaurs were a huge group of

dinosaurs. All of them were plant eaters, and all had broad, flattened

Hadrosaurs *had a great variety of crests, horns, knobs, and other structures on their heads. They were the most common family of dinosaurs.*

mouths. Because their flattened mouths were completely toothless in the front, they became known as the duck-billed dinosaurs.

It appears that hadrosaurs traveled in groups. A group was made up of several families that stayed together. They ate, slept, laid eggs, and raised their young together. Sticking together in a group would have provided some safety for these dinosaurs. They were not fierce meat eaters, and they were not good fighters. But in a group, they could warn each other of danger, protect their young, and band together to scare off attackers.

Scientists have found hadrosaur fossils all over the world. They have found footprints, eggs, nests, babies, and adults. They have found skeletal remains in North and South America, Europe, Asia, and even Antarctica. At one time, hadrosaurs were among the most common dinosaurs in the world.

CHAPTER SIX

BIG CHANGES AT THE K-T BOUNDARY

Edmontosaurus and all of the other dinosaurs died out around 65 million years ago. This was at the end of a time period called the Cretaceous (kree-TAY-shuss) period. It was also the beginning of the Tertiary (TER-shee-AIR-ee) period. This point in time is often called the K-T **boundary.** The *K* comes from the German word *Kreide* for "Cretaceous." The *T* stands for "Tertiary."

Although no one is certain why the dinosaurs

Dromaeosaurus *(DRO-mee-oh-SAWR-uhss) was a dinosaur that also lived in Alberta, Canada, during the Cretaceous period. Unlike* Edmontosaurus, *however,* Dromaeosaurus *was a meat eater.*

suddenly died out, some think that a giant **asteroid** is to blame.

Many scientists believe that a huge asteroid slammed into the earth

65 million years ago. The impact caused tons of dust and rock to fly

up into the air. The sky was darkened, and plants could no longer

grow. Plant-eating animals died out. And the animals that ate them

perished soon after. Land animals were not the only ones to vanish.

Many types of sea creatures disappeared as well.

Reptiles had ruled during the Cretaceous period. They were

absolutely everywhere. They ranged in size from tiny lizards to

mighty dinosaurs. But at the K-T boundary, things changed. The

dinosaurs disappeared forever, along with most other reptiles.

Many mammals vanished as well. However, during the Tertiary

period, many new mammals appeared. At the K-T boundary, the

Age of Reptiles truly ended and the Age of Mammals began.

Glossary

ancient (AYN-shunt) Something that is ancient is very old. Paleontologists study ancient life.

asteroid (ASS-tuh-roid) An asteroid is a rocky mass that is smaller than a planet and orbits the sun. Dinosaurs such as *Edmontosaurus* may have disappeared after an asteroid hit the earth.

boundary (BOUN-duh-ree) A boundary is a border or limit. *Edmontosaurus* died at a point in time known as the K-T boundary.

flexible (FLEK-suh-buhl) Something that is flexible bends easily. *Edmontosaurus*'s tail was not very flexible.

interpreted (in-TUR-prit-ed) To have interpreted something is to have decided what something means. The warning calls of birds are loud and short so they can be interpreted quickly.

reptile (REP-tile) A reptile is an animal that breathes air, has a backbone, and is usually covered with scales or plates. *Edmontosaurus* was a reptile.

sheath (SHEETH) A sheath is a covering. *Edmontosaurus*'s upper lip was protected by a sheath.

specimen (SPESS-uh-muhn) A specimen is a sample that is used to represent an entire group. The mummified *Edmontosaurus* specimen was discovered in 1909.

Did You Know?

▸ *Tyrannosaurus rex* hunted *Edmontosaurus*. We know this because *Edmontosaurus* bones have been found in *T. rex* droppings.

▸ An *Edmontosaurus* was the first dinosaur skeleton to be shown at the Smithsonian Institution, which is now famous for its amazing collection of prehistoric animal fossils.

▸ At one time, scientists thought that *Edmontosaurus* lived in the water and used its huge tail to swim.

How to Learn More

AT THE LIBRARY

Lambert, David, Darren Naish, and Liz Wyse. *Dinosaur Encyclopedia*.
New York: DK Publishing, 2001.

ON THE WEB

Visit our home page for lots of links about *Edmontosaurus*:

http://www.childsworld.com/links.html

NOTE TO PARENTS, TEACHERS, AND LIBRARIANS: We routinely verify our Web links
to make sure they're safe, active sites—so encourage your readers to check them out!

PLACES TO VISIT OR CONTACT

AMERICAN MUSEUM OF NATURAL HISTORY
To view numerous dinosaur fossils, including the
Edmontosaurus *mummy, as well as the fossils of*
several ancient mammals
Central Park West at 79th Street
New York, NY 10024-5192
212/769-5100

CARNEGIE MUSEUM OF NATURAL HISTORY
To view a variety of dinosaur skeletons, as well
as fossils related to other extinct animals
4400 Forbes Avenue
Pittsburgh, PA 15213
412/622-3131

DINOSAUR NATIONAL MONUMENT
To view a huge deposit of dinosaur bones
in a natural setting
Dinosaur, CO 81610-9724
           or
DINOSAUR NATIONAL MONUMENT (QUARRY)
11625 East 1500 South
Jensen, UT 84035
435/781-7700

MUSEUM OF THE ROCKIES
To see real dinosaur fossils, as well as robotic replicas
Montana State University
600 West Kagy Boulevard
Bozeman, MT 59717-2730
406/994-2251 or 406/994-DINO (3466)

NATIONAL MUSEUM OF NATURAL HISTORY
(SMITHSONIAN INSTITUTION)
To see several dinosaur exhibits and
special behind-the-scenes tours
10th Street and Constitution Avenue NW
Washington, DC 20560-0166
202/357-2700

The Geologic Time Scale

CAMBRIAN PERIOD
Date: 540 million to 505 million years ago
Most major animal groups appeared by the end of this period. Trilobites were common and algae became more diversified.

ORDOVICIAN PERIOD
Date: 505 million to 440 million years ago
Marine life became more diversified. Crinoids and blastoids appeared, as did corals and primitive fish. The first land plants appeared. The climate changed greatly during this period—it began as warm and moist, but temperatures ultimately dropped. Huge glaciers formed, causing sea levels to fall.

SILURIAN PERIOD
Date: 440 million to 410 million years ago
Glaciers melted, sea levels rose, and the earth's climate became more stable. Fish with jaws first appeared, as did the first freshwater fish. Plants with vascular systems developed. This means they had parts that helped them to conduct food and water.

DEVONIAN PERIOD
Date: 410 million to 360 million years ago
Fish became more diverse, as did land plants. The first trees and forests appeared at this time, and the earliest seed-bearing plants began to grow. The first land-living vertebrates and insects appeared. Fossils also reveal evidence of the first ammonites and amphibians. The climate was warm and mild.

CARBONIFEROUS PERIOD
Date: 360 million to 286 million years ago
The climate was warm and humid, but cooled toward the end of the period. Coal swamps dotted the landscape, as did a multitude of ferns. The earliest reptiles walked the earth. Pelycosaurs such as *Edaphosaurus* evolved toward the end of the Carboniferous period.

PERMIAN PERIOD
Date: 286 million to 248 million years ago
Algae, sponges and corals were common on the ocean floor. Amphibians and reptiles were also prevalent at this time, as were seed-bearing plants and conifers. However, this period ended with the largest mass extinction on earth. This may have been caused by volcanic activity or the formation of glaciers and the lowering of sea levels.

TRIASSIC PERIOD
Date: 248 million to 208 million years ago
The climate during this period was warm and dry. The first true mammals appeared, as did frogs, salamanders, and lizards. Evergreen trees made up much of the plant life. The first dinosaurs, including *Coelophysis*, walked the earth. In the skies, pterosaurs became the earliest winged reptiles to take flight. In the seas, ichthyosaurs and plesiosaurs made their appearance.

JURASSIC PERIOD

Date: 208 million to 144 million years ago

The climate of the Jurassic period was warm and moist. The first birds appeared at this time, and plant life was more diverse and widespread. Although dinosaurs didn't even exist in the beginning of the Triassic period, they ruled the earth by Jurassic times. *Allosaurus, Apatosaurus, Archaeopteryx, Brachiosaurus, Compsognathus, Diplodocus, Ichthyosaurus, Plesiosaurus,* and *Stegosaurus* were just a few of the prehistoric creatures that lived during this period.

CRETACEOUS PERIOD

Date: 144 million to 65 million years ago

The climate of the Cretaceous period was fairly mild. Many modern plants developed, including those with flowers. With flowering plants came a greater diversity of insect life. Birds further developed into two types: flying and flightless. Prehistoric creatures such as *Ankylosaurus, Edmontosaurus, Iguanodon, Maiasaura, Oviraptor, Psittacosaurus, Spinosaurus, Triceratops, Troodon, Tyrannosaurus rex,* and *Velociraptor* all existed during this period. At the end of the Cretaceous period came a great mass extinction that wiped out the dinosaurs, along with many other groups of animals.

TERTIARY PERIOD

Date: 65 million to 1.8 million years ago

Mammals were extremely diversified at this time, and modern-day creatures such as horses, dogs, cats, bears, and whales developed.

QUATERNARY PERIOD

Date: 1.8 million years ago to today

Temperatures continued to drop during this period. Several periods of glacial development led to what is known today as the Ice Age. Prehistoric creatures such as glyptodonts, mammoths, mastodons, *Megatherium,* and sabre-toothed cats roamed the earth. A mass extinction of these animals occurred approximately 10,000 years ago. The first human beings evolved during the Quaternary period.

Index

About the Author

Susan H. Gray has bachelor's and master's degrees in zoology and has taught college-level courses in biology. She first fell in love with fossil hunting while studying paleontology in college. In her 25 years as an author, she has written many articles for scientists and researchers, and many science books for children. Susan enjoys gardening, traveling, and playing the piano. She and her husband, Michael, live in Cabot, Arkansas.